how to have fun with
needlepoint

By Editors of Creative

Illustrated by Nan Brooks

DEDICATED TO
TOM, MIKE, KRISTY and TIMMY

creative
craft
book

Library of Congress Number: 73-18226
ISBN: 0-87191-296-1

Published by Creative Education, Mankato, Minnesota 56001. Distributed by Childrens Press, 1224 West Van Buren Street, Chicago, Illinois 60607

Library of Congress Cataloging in Publication Data
Creative Educational Society, Mankato, MN
    How to have fun with needlepoint.
                (Creative craft books)
    SUMMARY: Introduces basic needlepoint stitches and simple projects such as a hot mat and patches for jeans.
    1. Canvas embroidery — Juvenile literature.
(1. Canvas embroidery.   2. Needlework)   I. Title
TT778.C3C73 1973   746.4'4   73-18226
ISBN 0-87191-296-1

ED·WARD REX: V

ABOUT NEEDLEPOINT

Needlepoint is a form of embroidery. Embroidery is the oldest way to sew decorations on fabric. Articles with embroidered borders were done in Ancient Egypt, Greece, and Rome. Some of the richest examples of embroidery appear in the church hangings made during the Middle Ages.

Even though there are many different cultures and materials, embroidery throughout the world is very similar! Hundreds of variations have been developed, but the basic stitches of embroidery are the same.

The Pilgrims brought embroidery to America. As America developed many new embroidery variations and designs were created.

Today needlepoint is one of the most popular forms of embroidery. Needlepoint canvas can be purchased with only a background to fill in. Complete needlepoint kits with all of the materials and a canvas already stamped with a pattern are available. And, you can still make your own designs on regular canvas.

LET'S BEGIN

It is fun and easy to learn to needlepoint. You will need special materials to needlepoint but should not have trouble locating any of them. Now that needlepoint is so popular, materials are available almost everywhere.

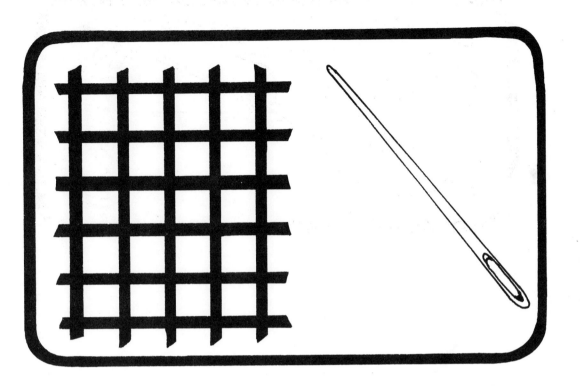

The first item you will need is a canvas. The size of the canvas is decided by the number of open squares (called mesh) to each inch. Try to get a canvas with 10 open squares to the inch. This is the easiest size canvas to learn on. A mono canvas will have one thread going up and one thread going across each square. Look at the picture of the mono canvas so you know for sure what you are looking for.

Next you need a tapestry needle. A tapestry needle will have a rounded tip that is not sharp like a regular sewing needle. They are made in different sizes. You should use an 18, 19, or 20 when learning to needlepoint.

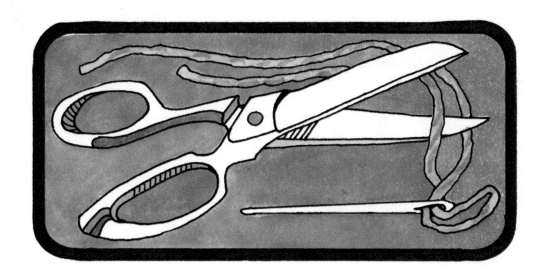

A pair of sharp scissors is important. Be careful with these. Remember not to leave your scissors or needle out so that someone can get hurt.

Many kinds and colors of yarn are available. A regular needlepoint yarn is made but if the color you want is not available in the needlepoint yarn select another kind of yarn. The only thing you must be careful of is that your yarn is not too thick for the canvas. If the yarn is too thick it will wear thin from being pulled through the squares.

Cut the yarn in strands that are about 12 to 18 inches long. The length of the strands of yarn is important. If it is too long it will be difficult for you to pull in and out. If it is too short you will have too many ends on the wrong side. Try to keep the wrong side of your canvas as neat as possible.

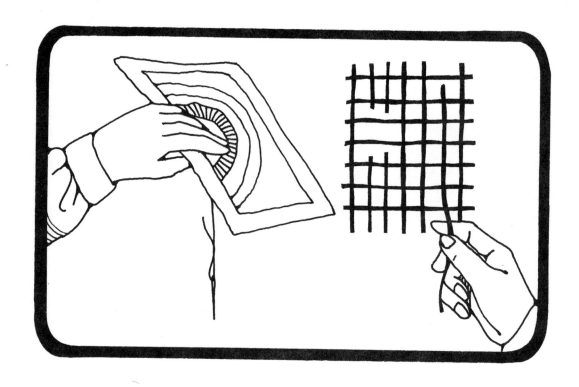

Now for a few quick pieces of information and on to needlepoint fun!

Your strand will become twisted when you are working. Hold your canvas up and let your needle hang free until it unwinds. Be sure to untwist your yarn as you work. Unless you do this your canvas will not be covered with neat, even stitches.

When you make a mistake either rip out the stitches using your scissors or pull the yarn and needle back through the squares. Then re-do. Be careful not to cut your canvas if you use the scissors to rip out.

If a thread comes out of your canvas, remove one from the bottom and work it into the broken area by weaving over and under.

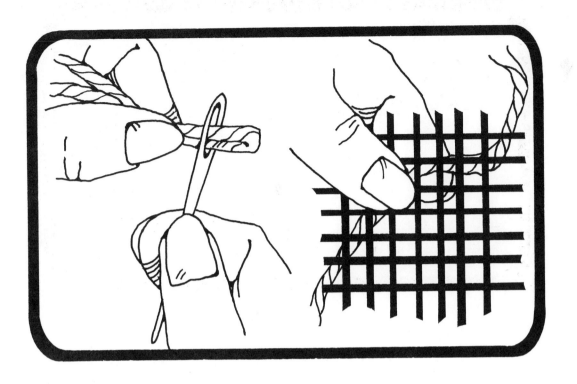

Let's begin by threading the needle. Hold the needle in your right hand between your thumb and finger. Make a fold in the yarn. Put the folded piece of yarn into the eye of your needle. Pull the yarn through until the needle is about 3 inches from the end. Do not put a knot in the end of your yarn. Knots are not used in needlepoint.

When you bring the needle up through the canvas to begin your first stitch, leave about an inch of loose yarn at the back of the canvas. Hold this yarn with your left hand at the back of the canvas. When you begin to needlepoint, put your stitches over the loose end. This will cover the loose end on the back side.

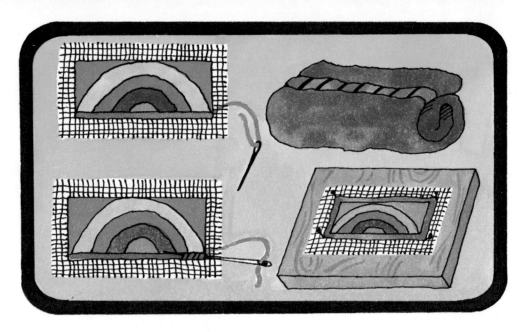

Always stop when you have about 2 inches of yarn left. When you have reached the end of a row, or have about 2 inches left on your strand of yarn, pull it through the last four stitches you made. Pull it until the yarn is tight. Cut the remaining yarn so that no ends show.

Sometimes your canvas will get stretched out of shape as you needlepoint. Don't worry about this. When you have completed your project, find a heavy towel. Wet the towel and roll your canvas up inside the towel. Leave the canvas inside the towel until the entire piece of needlepoint is damp.

Now you will need a piece of wood and tacks. Stretch the damp canvas on the board and tack down. Stretch it so that all sides are even when measured with a ruler. Leave the canvas stretched until it is completely dry.

14

EASY NEEDLEPOINT STITCHES

You might want to practice these needlepoint stitches on a piece of gingham cloth rather than on canvas. The gingham is made in checks like a piece of canvas.

There are many, many needlepoint stitches. We will learn only a couple of stitches. You will be able to complete needlepoint projects once you learn these stitches. Later, you can learn others.

15

16

The most common needlepoint stitch is a group of four stitches called the TENT STITCH. This stitch slants upward from the left to the right of the canvas. The four tent stitches all look the same on the front side of the canvas. It is only by looking at the wrong side that you will be able to tell the stitches apart. The Continental and Half-Cross are the most popular tent stitches. The Continental stitch is used more because it fills the background in evenly on the front and back side of the canvas. It is also a very firm and long lasting stitch. The Half-Cross stitch does not use as much yarn as the Continental. It is very fast to work. This cannot be worked on a mono canvas. It must be worked on the double-thread canvas.

The other two tent stitches are the Basket-Weave stitch and the Diagonal stitch.

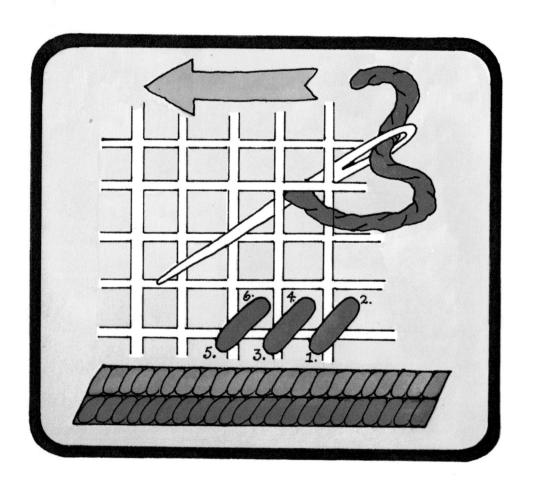

Let's begin with the Continental stitch. Start in the upper right corner of your canvas. Work all rows from right to left. Bring the needle up at the corner marked 1 on the diagram. Put it down at the corner of the square marked 2. Bring it up again at 3 and then down again at 4. Continue doing this to the end of the row. End your yarn at the end of the row. Now, do the second row the same as you did the first. Continue working in the Continental stitch until you are sure you understand it.

There are over one hundred different needlepoint stitches and variations. You can now do one of the tent stitches. Now you will want to learn a couple of the pattern stitches. Pattern stitches will help you make the many different needlepoint looks. Start with these. Later, you can learn others you might want to try.

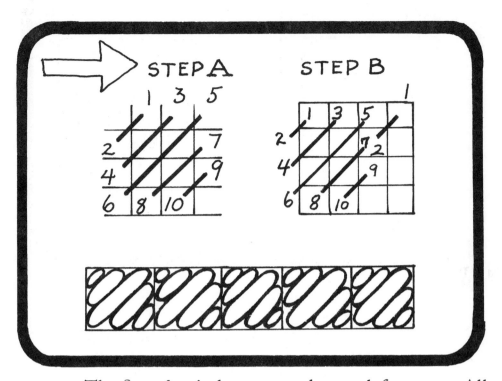

The Scotch stitch starts at the top left corner. All rows are worked from left to right. There are five stitches of different lengths in a square. Bring your needle up at 1. Put it down at 2. Bring it up at 3, down at 4 and up again at 5. Down again at 6. Up again at 7, down again at 8. Up again at 9, down again at 10. You have now completed the first Scotch stitch square. To begin the next square, follow the numbers 1 through 10 shown in Step B. Continue until you reach the end of the row. End your yarn. Begin the next row. Practice this stitch until you can work it without any trouble. When you want an interesting change, between each square and each row, put a row of Continental stitches in a different color.

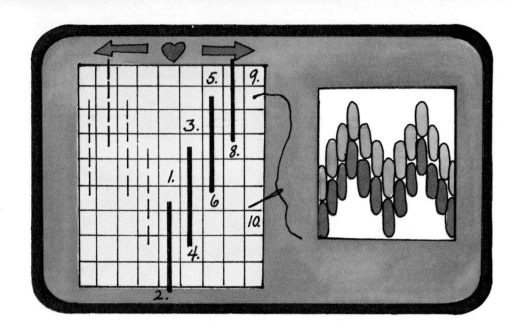

Now let's go on to the Florentine stitch. This is a very fast stitch and makes a very interesting design when worked in rows of different colors.

You must start this at the center of your canvas. Work each row from the center to the edge on both sides. Work up towards the top of your canvas. When you reach the top, turn the canvas around and work the other half towards the top.

Bring your needle up at Number 1. Go over three squares of the canvas, and then down at 2. Now bring your needle up at 3. This will leave one blank square between the 1 and 3. Down at 4. Up at 5, down at 6, up at 7, down at 8. Now, number 9 will be in line with 5 and 6. Number 11 with 3 and 4. Continue in this pattern until you reach the edge. Now work the left side the same way. Begin the second row using a different color.

NEEDLEPOINT PROJECTS

Once you have practiced these needlepoint stitches, you will be ready to make something using the stitches you know.

You will need a piece of number 10 mono canvas that is 7½ inches long by 7½ inches wide. A tapestry needle size 18. And three colors of yarn.

Mark with a pencil or marking pen a border that is ¾ of an inch from the outside of your canvas. This will make a square that is 6 inches.

Begin on the pencil line at the top. Begin with the Continental stitch. Do this in one color of the yarn you selected. Also do the bottom pencil line. Turn the canvas around so that you can work the other two pencil lines. This is your border.

Now find the center of your square. At this point begin working the Florentine stitch. When you have worked one row to both edges do the second row in another color. On the third row use the same color as the first row.

When you have reached the top turn the canvas around and do the bottom half.

Be sure to keep the top rows in the same pattern even though you will not be able to reach all the way.

When you have filled your square with the Florentine stitch, find a piece of felt for the back of your canvas. Make a cut into the corners of your canvas. Fold the canvas edges back and glue to the felt.

Now you have completed your first needlepoint project. This can be used on mom's table to set hot bowls and dishes on or it can be framed and hung on the wall. Have fun making these in as many different colors as you want. You can even do every row in a different color.

Until you have completed several projects you should keep your needlepoint projects very simple.

Something easy you can do is to make needlepoint patches for your jeans. First you must cut a piece of canvas that is about 2 inches larger than the place you want to cover. You can cut the canvas in different shapes and sizes.

You can either draw a design on your canvas or use your favorite stitch. Have fun making interesting designs and patches for your jeans. You can also get small frames for these and use them as pictures.

After you have completed the patch, cut the corners and glue the patch to the felt the same way you did for the larger piece. Now sew your patches on your jeans.

Have fun with all your needlepoint projects. Make them over and over and over before you decide to try other needlepoint stitches and projects.

how to have fun

BAKING COOKIES AND CAKES
BUILDING SAILBOATS
KNITTING
WITH MACRAME
MAKING BIRDHOUSES AND FEEDERS
MAKING BREAKFAST
MAKING CHRISTMAS DECORATIONS
MAKING KITES
MAKING MOBILES
MAKING PAPER AIRPLANES
MAKING PUPPETS
WITH NEEDLEPOINT
SEWING
WEAVING
WITH AN INDOOR GARDEN

creative craft books